3 4028 07851 6037
HARRIS COUNTY PUBLIC LIBRARY

DISCARD

D1411658

ISBN: 1450542646
ISBN-13: 9781450542647

To
My Father
ABDUL HAMEED KHAN

PREFACE

Ghalib was born in 1797 in Agra, India as Asadullah Khan, in the landed gentry in the dying days of the Mughal Empire, and remained financially well off for most of his life. He later moved to Delhi, the capital of the Mughal Empire, and soon became the favorite of the last Mughal king, himself a renowned poet. He was married at an early age and had seven children, none of whom survived. He died in Delhi, India in 1869 at the age of 72 years.

He started writing poetry in his teens under the pen names of Asad and Ghalib, and wrote mostly odes or ghazals in Persian and Urdu but, although he wrote less in Urdu, it was for his Urdu odes that he became famous and immortal. He wrote in the classical Eastern tradition, mainly about love and beauty but was also deep and philosophical.

Translation by its very nature cannot capture the taste and flavor of the original. It is not possible to translate the beat, the rhythm, and the flow in another language, and especially in English which is so different from Urdu. However, I have tried to preserve some of it by translating the couplets as couplets. Also, in the translation I have used the pen name of Ghalib only in order to avoid confusion.

Ghalib's love is primarily romantic and beauty feminine:

> *Oh, my gal is like the harvest moon*
> *And she has more shine than the sun at noon*

> *Yes, the moon looks lovely when it is full*
> *But she's always gorgeous and beautiful*

> *But like a garden in the moonlit night*
> *GHALIB, her face is a lover's delight*

> *When flies in the breeze her curly hair*
> *The musk of Tatar you smell everywhere*

1

Her brow is a bow; her glance a dart
She can jab, and stab, and wound your heart

Oh, the way she smiles and the way she winks
And her beautiful eyes the way she blinks

She's tall and slim like a cypress tree
And a riot she causes wherever is she

My heart is on fire; it is like hell
And she is a bombshell, that beautiful belle

But as is so typical of the beauties in the Eastern poetry, his gal is cruel and callous:

Oh, cruelty and malice, she has them all
But then she is also a beautiful doll

And whenever I am a little bit jealous
She becomes very spiteful, cruel, and callous

She wants not only my heart to bleed
But also my blood in my tears indeed

When I tell her I love her, she takes her dart
And goes on to test my poor little heart

And while she's sleeping, if I kiss her feet
She wakes up and tells me that I'm a cheat

My peace of mind she does subvert
She's so very coy; she's such a flirt

But love is not love if it is happy and successful; indeed it is bad, mad, and very, very sad:

You can't have love without the ache
Your heart must yearn; it also must break

With sorrow and pain though love is rife
Escape them you cannot; they're a part of life

O deadly and ruinous are the ways of desire
And the outlook for a lover is all too dire

From pain and suffering he cannot part
And the sorrow is always eating his heart

And though dying is hard for so many guys
Think how many times a poor lover dies

And she lives in Heaven, that infidel
While here I'm burning in the fire of hell

But Ghalib is philosophical and takes it in stride, and can even be a little funny:

Oh, what's a lover if he does not yearn
And what is a fire if it does not burn?

It's easier to hide in your clothes the fire
Than to hide in your heart a burning desire

An eternal bliss only death can claim
For life and sorrow are one and the same

And since nobody dies without a cause
Without reason, GHALIB, a lover can't go

The realm of beauty is without any bound
And it's love that makes the world go round

When the angels quiz me after my death
I wish they won't test for liquor my breath

> On the Judgment Day when angels I'll face
> I'll need a lawyer to plead my case

Ghalib can also be mystical when he wants to:

> O don't be stingy with the cup of mine
> For your heavenly vat has plenty of wine
>
> Yes, we're all topers: we drink very hard
> Even angels for us have a lot of regard
>
> At the sound of music we go in a trance
> We hear from God and dance and dance
>
> Oh, we're the observers, and we're the observed
> We see our backs, our sights are curved
>
> We think we're awake, or so it may seem
> But still we're dreaming while awake in a dream
>
> And I see in there the image divine
> Whether it's a temple, a mosque, or a shrine

And then he asks difficult questions, and finding no satisfactory answers, in the end he, as a strong believer in Hindu Maya or illusion, concludes:

> Oh, in Your being I have no doubt
> But tell me, O God, what is it all about?
>
> Why do we have these beautiful girls
> And what are the brows and the raven curls?
>
> And why do they have such charming eyes
> And why do they enchant and mesmerize?
>
> And what're the clouds, and what's the breeze
> And why are there flowers, bushes, and trees?

And why do the lovers hold them so dear
The girls who're faithless and insincere?

The reality of being is greatly in doubt
It's hard to know what it's all about

Oh, it is not so very difficult to guess
That everything ends in nothingness

And in the end there's nothing to explain
It's all subjective, this joy, this pain

So let's not have any more confusion
The world is naught; it's just an illusion

BUT ALL IS NOT LOST; THERE IS ALSO THE BRIGHT SIDE:

O with great fanfare the spring is here
And the moon and the stars are coming to cheer

The bounty of God you cannot deny
Oh, what a beautiful way to beautify?

With splendor the earth is flying high
It has become as dazzling as the glamorous sky

It's bright and beautiful, and happy, and gay
And everything is green, and gone is the gray

In the springtime rain, having taken their showers
The flowers are admiring their fellow flowers

The breeze is bursting with fragrance divine
And the air is drunk with the smell of wine

Khalid Hameed Shaida, MD
E.Mail: khalmeed@aol.com
Web: www.writing.com/authors/khalmeed

1

Naqsh faryaadi hay kis ki shoukhi e tehreer ka

O what has been written do not decry
And accept your fate; it's futile to cry

The nights are long, and lonely are you
Your life is hell; this you cannot deny

Her long eyelashes are like the swords
They are eager to kill and surely not shy

And whatever she says you can't understand
Her words are mysterious; they so mystify

And I know you're restive, O GHALIB my friend
But you are a captive of a charming eye

2

Juz Qais aur koie na aaya ba roo e kaar

In the dreadful wild only a lover can go
It's surely no place for his terrible foe

In a lover's breast there's nothing but fire
So when he breathes only smoke does flow

His joy comes only when he dreams of his love
For the rest of the time he has nothing but woe

He learns his lessons in the school of love
Only suffering and sorrow where he comes to know

In his grave he finds his only refuge
For it covers his faults from head to toe

And since nobody dies without a cause
Without reason, GHALIB, a lover can't go

3
Kehtay ho na daen gay hum dil ager parha paaya

If she found my heart, she won't give it back
She says she'll keep it with her bric-a-brac

These pangs of love one has to endure
With so many doctors only she has the cure

My sighing and crying have lost their effect
But my rivals are happy; that's what they expect

I have acted smart; I have acted dumb
But matters it little; she thinks I'm a bum

Oh, when in the spring the flowers bloom
My heart does bleed; it's filled with gloom

With this crazy heart I would love to part
And she's welcome to keep if she finds my heart

And although he thinks that he's being nice
I wish the preacher wouldn't give me advice

4

Dil mera soaz e nihaan say bai mahaaba jal gaya

Oh, I'm in love; my heart is on fire
And it has consumed my being entire

The wreckage of my heart is so complete
That it has no memory, no hope, no desire

My flaming sighs could consume the world
But now I'm nothing; my condition is dire

And once I could also light up the town
With my raging fire and my burning desire

I could also reduce the wild to ashes
By simply intending there to retire

And even though, GHALIB, I'm all burnt out
The pity of the world I'll never require

5

Shouq her rang raqeeb e ser o saamaan nikla

O deadly and ruinous are the ways of desire
And the outlook for a lover is all too dire

The plight of his heart is so very bad
That when it hits it, the dart feels sad

And whether it's smoke, or a sigh, or a cry
A lover in trouble they all signify

From pain and suffering he cannot part
And the sorrow is always eating his heart

And though dying is hard for so many guys
Think how many times a poor lover dies

And, GHALIB, when a lover sheds tears of blood
How drop by drop he produces a flood

6
Dhamki maen mer gaya na jo baab e naburd tha

The pain of love only a he man can take
For even a giant its rigor can break

A lover must live in the shadow of death
So don't say a thing; you'll waste your breath

The code of fidelity he simply must follow
And a lot of insults he just has to swallow

To see his gal, oh, how much he needs
But she wounds his heart and it bleeds and bleeds

In his poor little heart there's nothing but pain
And even when it dies, the pain does remain

A lover's madness there's no way to cure
You can put him in chains but it's never secure

And, GHALIB, when he dies, how people cry
And say, by Jove he was quite a guy

7

Dehr maen naqsh e wafa wajh e tasalli na hua

To the people devotion is a useless word
And fidelity sounds so totally absurd

To touch those locks I do not dare
So proud and haughty is her curly hair

To kill my pain I wanted to die
But she wants me to live and cry and cry

So to live with sorrow, I began to think
I should give up my piety and drink and drink

And if she doesn't promise to come back to me
It's no use insisting; I should just let it be

I shouldn't be complaining about my fate
And if I cannot die, I simply must wait

So, GHALIB, with pain I have learnt to cope
And of my being revived there is no hope

8

Sataaishger hay zaahid is qader jis baagh e Rizwaan ka

The garden that the preacher calls paradise
It is simply for him a luring device

When the long eyelashes dig blood from the hearts
It shines like rubies on the tips of their darts

In moaning and groaning I'm so very astute
That when I am crying, I sound like a flute

The fire in my heart is quite a sight
It lights up the world, it burns so bright

Her shining face to my tears can do
What does the sun to the drops of dew

Oh, when I'm lonely, I begin to dread
That like a mad farmer I'll burn my shed

My wisdom and prudence I simply fling
And head for the desert when comes the spring

With my dying desires I become lovesick
And burn very quietly like a candlestick

And my darling gal I cannot forget
And if it's too much, I've no regret

But when with my rival she goes and sleeps
I just can't stand it; it gives me the creeps

But on her lashes when I see those tears
I so want to kiss them; my rage disappears

Oh, GHALIB, I'm tired; I want to die
And to all my woes to say good-bye

9

Mehram naheen hay too hi nawaha e raaz ka

The Heavenly mystery you think you know
And you think, O preacher, you're the only pro

My friend, you should see the glory of dawn
When the flowers all smile and say - come on!

And of night when girls entice young men
And lovers just watch with yearning and yen

These hapless lovers just bear and grin
Though breathe they fire with great chagrin

And watch the bar where the bubbly wine
Those beauties drink, and look so divine

And men their love to the girls declare
While gently untying their knotted hair

But for lovers, GHALIB, there is no cure
Their pain of parting they just have to endure

10
Bazm e shaahinshaaha maen ashaar ka dafter khula

The court of the king has poets galore
May the culture flourish more and more

It's a sacred temple and a shining star
Which they come to admire from near and far

When comes my gal to take my life
She comes equipped with a dagger and a knife

And although my girl is awfully mysterious
She's also very sensuous which makes me curious

For the beautiful gals I so much crave
That houris I'll find when I enter my grave

Her veil my gal doesn't have to wear
She can hide her face with her curly hair

Oh, once she said I could live in her street
But then she ignored me, and refused to meet

And though I think it sounds bizarre
My pain and sorrow are due to my star

I feel like a stranger without a home
And aimlessly here I'm born to roam

But master my fate I feel I can
For, GHALIB, I am a Mohammedan

11

Shab keh burq e soaz e dil say zehra e abr aab tha

With my fiery heart in such a form
My flowing tears are causing a storm

She says she cannot come in the rain
For my crying had caused a hurricane

She makes me cry, that callous girl
For her a tear is much like a pearl

My tears of blood are a source of glee
For jewels and rubies she likes to see

And while she's sleeping in a cozy bed
She wants me to cry and bang my head

With my awful rivals she loves to play
While I sit and watch in great dismay

And she lives in Heaven, that infidel
While here I'm burning in the fire of hell

And with a charming look she throws a dart
That jabs, and stabs, and wounds my heart

And her my rivals when they try to seduce
My howling and crying are of no use

And then I shed the tears of blood
And with my tears I cause a flood

My poverty and need I don't try to hide
For in lofty thoughts I take great pride

And although people think that I'm mad
I feel so great; it's not at all bad

For this captive now she does not care
But there was a time when she was loving and fair

And though she was a predator and I a prey
She used to pursue me night and day

But GHALIB tells me I shouldn't cry
Because I can drown the earth and the sky

12

Aek aek qatray ka mujhay daena parha hisaab

Every drop of blood in my heart does belong
To her charming eyes and their lashes long

Her image I used to keep in my heart
But now with my heart she has taken it apart

Oh, I love it so much that if I could
I would ask to be buried in her neighborhood

There isn't a desert without a mirage
And everywhere in love there's camouflage

But about love, GHALIB, I shouldn't complain
Because life itself is so full of pain

13
Bus keh dushwaar hay her kaam ka aasaan hona

It's not, I know, so easy to attain
But I do wish humans were a little humane

My love is crazy; in the desert I roam
I've destroyed my life, and ruined my home

I so want to see her, whatever the cost
But when I've a chance, I'm completely lost

When she looks at me, I'm hit by a dart
And with her long eyelashes she stabs my heart

But when she comes to take my life
I cannot wait to give her a knife

For her rosy face I yearn and crave
But my yearnings and cravings will go in my grave

Oh, how I love her every little fault
And need in my wounds a little bit of salt

But sadly my gal is not very bright
For only after killing she feels contrite

So GHALIB says I shouldn't tear my hair
For to my balding head I'm not being fair

14

Dost ghamkhaari maen maeri seie fermaaen gay kya

O friends, your sympathy is of no use
My pain and sorrow I myself produce

She's splendid and proud, and cares she not
And whatever I say, she says - so what?

I always tell her that I want to die
But she wouldn't kill me; she wants me to cry

Our preacher is always giving me advice
But I wish he would also say something nice

And he also tells me I'm too insane
To be restrained by any rope or chain

And when I ask to be put in a jailer's care
He tells me I'm a prisoner of her curly hair

Oh, for love in Delhi people don't care
So, GHALIB, I'll leave and go elsewhere

15

Yeh na thi hamaari qismat keh wisaal e yaar hota

Oh, it's my destiny; oh, it's my fate
To meet my gal I've to wait and wait

She keeping her word I cannot conceive
I would die of joy if I could only believe

She promised and promised but never came
When asked, the excuse she made was lame

You should come and see how she throws her dart
And how it goes and wounds the heart

I wish my friends wouldn't give me advice
But give me some sympathy, which would be nice

For the pangs of love are a different breed
They can take a stone and make it bleed

With sorrow and pain though love is rife
Escape them you cannot; they're a part of life

But there's nothing worse than the parting pain
Oh, how it kills you again and again

I wish I'm swallowed by an ocean wave
Then I won't have a funeral; I won't have a grave

But during my life a girl I'll seek
Who is simply precious and totally unique

And GHALIB tells me some people think
That I would be a saint if I didn't drink

16
Hawas ko hay nishaat e kaar kya kya

An eternal life we'll all like to grab
But life without death will be dull and drab

To love and fidelity, in sharp contrast
Our lust is fleeting and does not last

Oh, a lover can venture; a lover can dare
But he has no patience; he cannot forbear

For the scent in the air I do not care
The fragrance of her dress I can smell everywhere

Oh, the maid of the bar when she gives me a glance
I need no wine to go into a trance

About my pain she doesn't want to know
And even when I tell her, she only says - oh!

But when she's kind, I lose my pain
I feel so happy I forget to complain

And when she gives me a saucy look
I feel very certain that I'm on the hook

Oh how she controls my every emotion
For I'm only a drop, and she is the ocean

And when she comes to take my life
With a look she does it; she needs no knife

And then I beg her not to depart
And listen to the timbre of my breaking heart

She makes a promise, and throws me a bait
But comes she does not, and I wait and wait

And when she flirts, she's very, very coy
And, GHALIB, to her I'm only a toy

17
Derkhur e qahr o ghazab jab koie hum saa na hua

The cruelty and pain that I have to endure
For them I was made, I feel quite sure

But even in bondage I feel very free
I won't go to Mecca if I didn't agree

But God is one and the only one
And among the idols like Him is none

And there's nothing more charming than a beautiful eye
Its power to enchant nobody can deny

My pain is useless if I do not moan
What use is my sorrow if it remains unknown?

I moan and groan, and I sob and sigh
For no one does suffer as much as I

To tell my story when I do proceed
I make the hearts of my listeners bleed

And if in a drop you can't see an ocean
Of God and man you have no notion

And even though, GHALIB, in love I crashed
I was so very lucky I didn't get smashed

18
Paay nazr e karam tohfa hay sharm e naarasaaie ka

O virtue and piety I do not claim
I'm begging for mercy; I've nothing but shame

My girl is beautiful but not sincere
But don't tell her that; she doesn't want to hear

Like the morning sun is her radiant face
It can fill your place with beauty and grace

For love and friendship she does not care
And if you love her, you'll die of despair

I so want to talk but cannot speak
I feel so helpless; I feel so weak

You know that I do not teach or preach
But colorful flowers I can put in my speech

And though my faults you cannot condone
That she can't be trusted is also well known

And, GHALIB, I'm lonesome as I can be
And this pain of parting is killing me

19

Ger na andoh e shab e furqat bayaan ho jay ga

If the pain of parting I do not show
That I miss her so much she'd never know

Without her nights are so terribly dark
That even the moon looks bleak and stark

And while she's sleeping, if I kiss her feet
She wakes up and tells me that I'm a cheat

When I tell her I love her, she takes her dart
And goes on to test my poor little heart

And when she's nice, I somehow find
That the world has also become very kind

But when she's severe, she tells me to forbear
So I control my fire and grin and bear

When I go to the park, the flowers take heed
And seeing my plight they start to bleed

And when with my sorrow I cannot cope
On the Day of Judgment I pin my hope

So everything, GHALIB, is as it was
And mine is truly a hopeless cause

20
Dard minnatkash e dawa na hua

My pain can't be helped, not even a tad
And if I'm not better, it's not so bad

Oh, how I wish she would use a knife
And stab my heart and take my life

My wound is old, but it bleeds and bleeds
It seems on itself it feeds and feeds

But to ask her to come I would not dare
For in my house there's not even a chair

She came to rob and not to stay
And snatched my heart and went away

She likes my rivals because they're obtuse
And they take from her a lot of abuse

In front of my rivals she fights with me
And they so much enjoy my tragedy

Look, she was my goddess, and I was her slave
But alas to me not a thing she gave

But my Maker made me and gave me a lot
And how His kindness I promptly forgot

So, things, you see, are getting worse
We miss you, GHALIB; come read your verse

21

Gila hay shouq ko dil maen bhee tangi e ja ka

My heart containing my surging emotion
Is like an oyster holding an ocean

I write and write, and try and try
But she to my letters does not reply

After every winter there comes the spring
And joy do pain and sorrow bring

When the pain of her absence does overpower
I don't want to see a smiling flower

But when her beauty I go to pry
My every pore does become an eye

The moment I saw her I could not part
And could not wait to give her my heart

With a yearning heart, and hopes, and fears
A terrible flood can cause my tears

And, GHALIB, I love her; she's my queen
And for me her tyranny is quite routine

22

Yak zarra e zameen naheen baikaar baagh ka

Without the flowers a garden is naught
And a tulip is nothing without its spot

Oh, life is painful without the wine
And a barman's offer is hard to decline

This love is madness, O nightingale
See, the flowers laugh whenever you wail

So, therefore, I go and write my verse
And myself in it I completely immerse

And though I have tried again and again
From loving the girls I cannot abstain

Our love wants blood, both yours and mine
Just like in a bar a lover wants wine

But like a garden in a moonlit night
GHALIB, her face is a lover's delight

23

Wo meri cheen e jabeen say gham e pinhaan samjha

By the looks of me you can guess my pains
For the title can tell what a book contains

My heart is broken; oh, I'm in despair
Do something please; I'm tearing my hair

My pain has made my heart so glum
That a dungeon dark it has now become

Oh, when I see her taking a stroll
My love for her gets out of control

My girl is saucy, and I'm so tame
And to my hay she's like a flame

In my journey of love I've become so weak
That a place of rest I always seek

Oh, I'm afraid of her long eyelashes
For my heart is full of jabs and slashes

And though, GHALIB, she's a beautiful belle
She is also a faithless infidel

24
Phir mujhay deeda e tar yaad aaya

Oh, when I remembered her tearful eye
I really thought I was going to die

And when she said she wanted to go
To my poor little heart it came as a blow

My silly old heart, I don't know why
It's always looking for a charming eye?

Its foolish desires I can't satisfy
Oh, I'm so tired I can't even cry

Why fell I in love I do not know?
I was quite alright; it didn't have to be so

But even in Heaven if I went for good
I'll never forget her neighborhood

Oh, I'm sick, and tired, and all alone
I cannot even cry, or moan, or groan

And when I go to look for my heart
It's in her alley that I make a start

And when in a desert I go to roam
I'm always reminded of my deserted home

And do you know, GHALIB, when I was a boy
Stoning the lovers I used to enjoy?

25

Hoie taakheer toe kuchh baais e taakheer bhee tha

Oh, whenever you came to this silly hack
Someone was always holding you back

Not all's your fault, my lovely mate
A part of the problem is also my fate

And if you've forgotten, I'd like to say
That once, when hunting, I became your prey

And though as a captive I like to complain
Of your golden braid I so love the chain

Your lightening words, they give me a shock
But, darling, I love to hear you talk

You've beauty of Joseph whenever I say
You feel so slighted that I feel dismay

Oh, I love to see my rivals try
And not succeed and cry and cry

I know I'm crazy; my plight is sad
But I'm like Romeo, and he was mad

I'm willing to die; so use your dart
And let it go and strike my heart

On the Judgment Day when angels I'll face
I'll need a lawyer to plead my case

He's the master of Urdu, this GHALIB I know
But you know poet Meer, he was also a pro

26
Too dost kisi ka bhee sitamger na hua tha

Everyone loves her but loves she none
In this my rivals and I are one

Oh, my gal is like the harvest moon
And she has more shine than the sun at noon

I've lost my courage; I've lost my power
But tears like pearls I still can shower

She's tall and slim like a cypress tree
And a riot she causes wherever is she

And when she gives me sorrow and pain
I'm strangely happy; I do not complain

On the mercy of God I totally rely
For no one has sinned as much as I

And the fire of love that burns in my soul
On it, O GHALIB, I have no control

27
Arz e niyaaz e ishq kay qaabil naheen raha

It has lost its fire; it has lost its glow
What happened to my heart, I do not know

For whatever happened there's no one to blame
But I'm losing fire; I'm a dying flame

She wouldn't even agree to take my life
For it is not worth soiling her knife

Oh, it's hard to believe, and it's so sad
But she cannot distinguish between good and bad

To see her beauty although I'm free
I get so dazzled that I cannot see

And though I'm crushed by sorrow and pain
From thinking of her I cannot refrain

And though I've lost my wish and desire
To see her with luck I still conspire

And, GHALIB, though beauty I still admire
My woeful heart has lost its fire

28
Zikr us paariwash ka aur phir bayaan apna

When I talk of her beauty, as I usually do
I can make my friends my rivals too

Drinking with my foes when got she drunk
Herself she was testing and she did flunk

Up there I know there is many a heaven
But I want a number that's higher than seven

She said she'll come but won't be alone
But luckily I'm friendly with her chaperone

When I said I'll write my sorry tale
She said my hands are just too frail

When I said I'll go and kiss her door
She said I will only dirty her floor

But it's good to know that I'm not insane
For about her my foes do also complain

So, GHALIB, there's a lot I can tolerate
But what do I do with my cruel fate

29

Ghaafil ba wahm e naaz khudaara hay werna yaan

If she decks herself, it's just out of pride
For she's known for her beauty far and wide

Don't go to the bar in search of ease
Your pain and sorrow it cannot appease

On the mercy of God if you totally rely
You will never be questioned after you die

Oh, if she kills me I would be glad
For this is a wish that I've always had

So my life, GHALIB, is for her to claim
For I am the moth, and she is the flame

30
Joer say baaz aa'ay per baaz aa'aen kya

Oh, it's so cruel when she hides her face
But she says it's not, which is a disgrace

I've decided to wait; I'm not in a hurry
And about what happens I'm not going to worry

She may be cruel, but she wants to be kind
So whatever she does, I really don't mind

When I write for her, I say it'll be better
If I went myself to deliver the letter

And if she ignores me, I'll let her ignore
But I'd like to stay close to her door

And I'm not afraid of saying good-bye
For all my life I've been waiting to die

But when she asks, who is GHALIB pray?
O please do tell me what do I say?

31
Ishrat e qatra hay darya maen fana ho jaana

I'm a drop of rain; I seek the ocean
When my pain is too much, it becomes the potion

For long we couldn't see eye to eye
When things got better, she said good-bye

The problems we had were all too knotty
And the progress we made was very, very spotty

And now she's as cold as she can be
And somehow she has stopped being cruel to me

Now instead of weeping I can only sigh
My tears I have learnt to gasify

Her painted nails O how can I forget?
They are red, and blue, and violet

My flowing tears when I can contain
The clouds disperse, and it stops to rain

When the scent of flowers goes into the air
It wants to reach and stay in her hair

And when in the spring it begins to rain
My clarity of judgment starts to wane

Then things of beauty I start to chase
And, GHALIB, I yearn to see her face

32
Phir hua waqt keh ho baalkusha moaj e sharaab

O the time is right, and the weather is fine
Let's bring the flask, and have some wine

It's softly raining, and the spring is here
Let's soak our souls with whisky and beer

Oh, some things in life are totally divine
The flowers, the sunset, the breeze, the wine

The tulips and roses in the park are drunk
And the grapes on the vine are full of spunk

What looks like blood in the veins of vine
Becomes in the bottle the spirit divine

As the color of flowers makes the garden bright
For the soul the wine is the source of light

And there's something that the wine does contain
That's good for the mind, and good for brain

And when it's green in the world everywhere
The wine does add something to the air

And if her lash can kill with a sting
In it the wine has the life spring

And he who sorrow in the wine can drown
Him luck does favor, and gives him the crown

The beautiful flowers give the world its color
And without the wine our lives would be duller

So, GHALIB, these flowers are simply divine
Go get the bottle and let's have some wine

33

Aamad e khat say hua hay sard jo bazaar e dost

Her beautiful cheeks are losing the glow
And lines on her face are beginning to show

To see her beauty although we're free
We're totally dazzled when we go and see

And when in the garden she takes a walk
People are astounded, and they simply gawk

And envy my rival oh, how I do
I feel I'm dying; I am so blue

I'm glad she's happy, this girl of mine
Although my blood she drinks like wine

And when I miss her, my rival pretends
That he and I are the best of friends

And says that he is a friend of my gal
And deliver my message to her he shall

And then he tells me about her hair
Knowing that it will cause me despair

And when he sees I am about to cry
Her beauty he starts to glorify

Oh, I cannot tell you which one is worse
The pang of my love or my rival's curse

But, GHALIB, your verses are a lover's abode
And this, my friend, is a beautiful ode

34

Nafas na anjuman e aarzoo say baaher khheench

O whatever you do, don't give up desire
For whatever you want, you can surely acquire

To see you once, my beautiful gal
Much pain and sorrow endure I shall

I wish my heart were calm and sedate
And not in a hurry, and willing to wait

And worry not about what people think
To spite my foes, with me you drink

O you're so beautiful, come throw your dart
And boldly jab and wound my heart

My heart is aflame with a burning desire
And like a kebab, it is sitting on fire

35

Husn ghamzay ki kashakash say chhuta maeray baad

O when I'm gone, they won't be so coy
And cruelty these girls will not enjoy

For their grace and charm no one will care
For a lover like me will never be there

And after me, yearning will simply choke
And the fire of love will be smothered by smoke

And beauties will stop painting their nails
And will hide their faces behind the veils

And put mascara they'll certainly not
And no one will show her beauty spot

And though a lover may still be insane
He'll surely not tear his clothes again

And my cup of wine no one will touch
And no one will dare to drink as much

In love not one will be as genuine
Nor at least as loyal as I have been

And not one, GHALIB, will take the blows
Nor handle like me the flood of woes

36

Bala say haen jo yeh paish e nazar dar o deewaar

O come and knock with all your grace
My door is dying to see your face

When I cry and cry, I flood the floor
With nothing but blood from door to door

Oh, when you come, in order to greet
My door jumps out, and goes to the street

And when you knock, it goes in a trance
And like a drunk it begins to dance

And when for long you don't come by
It's awake all night like a watchful eye

And when at night I cry and cry
It shuts itself, and says good-bye

And to live next door when you come to explore
My door, it wants to become next door

And if you don't come and show your face
It tells me to promptly demolish my place

And when I'm drowning in a sea of woe
My door feels happy, and says – oho!

And, GHALIB, something if I want to hide
I know, I cannot in my door confide

37
Gher jab bana lia tera der per kahay baghair

Since I've been mostly living at her door
She has been ignoring me more and more

She tells me always that though I'm weak
She can't know my wishes if I do not speak

How foolish of me that I've been amorous
About a gal who is cruel and callous

I'm a person who'll talk, come what may
But I just can't tell her what I want to say

I may go to Heaven; I may go to hell
But I'll always worship my infidel

A long eyelash, when it takes my life
I simply have to call it a dagger or a knife

And when I discuss the knowledge divine
I use the words like goblet and wine

I pretend to be deaf, for it's a device
By which I make her say things twice

But her, O GHALIB, you shouldn't haunt
For she knows exactly what you want

38
Kuin jal gaya na taab e rukh e yaar daekh ker

It's hard to believe that you would see
And dazzled by her you wouldn't be

Oh, when I'm aflame with a burning desire
Everyone suspects that I worship fire

The meaning of love, oh, how she perverts
And a hapless lover how badly she hurts

And when she comes to take my life
I almost die when I see her knife

The waves of wine in the cup she mocks
When drinking her wine, in the bar she walks

When she sees that cruelty I do not mind
To have a little fun, she becomes very kind

O I'll sell my body; I'll sell my soul
If in love I can possibly reach my goal

I'll give up faith, and piety, and creed
If I think I can in my love succeed

I'm so discouraged; I'm so lovelorn
To get my rose, I'll put up with thorn

But she's so suspicious and so unjust
That whatever I say she would not trust

Yes God, like Moses, I cannot observe
But seeing my goddess I surely deserve

So, GHALIB, you see, I cannot get ahead
For against a wall I 'm banging my head

39

Larazta hay mera dil zehmat e mehr e darakhshaan per

Like a drop of dew on a desert thorn
For death I wait for the sun in the morn

When the light went out of Jacob's eye
To the dungeon of Joseph it went to pry

I've known this, Romeo, since you were a boy
That you one day your love will destroy

If I cry and cry, it's not my fault
She's always rubbing in my wound the salt

Between a lover and a gal is a great divide
For the one has meekness and the other pride

Oh, when at dawn the sky is on fire
The pain of her absence is also very dire

When the lovers die and lie in the dust
Their wishes and urges remain robust

Whether I rip my clothes or tear my hair
O GHALIB, this pain I'll simply have to bear

40

Hay bus keh her ik un kay ishaaray maen nishaan aur

It's not so simple, she's very mysterious
She says she loves, but she is never serious

She doesn't understand what I impart
So change my tongue or change her heart

And when she wants to wound my heart
She needs no bow to throw her dart

And since she's in town, it's out of control
And everyone is hiding his heart and soul

To give up my idol I'll be the last
For I'm not surely an iconoclast

If I had more eyes to shed my blood
I'd have cried and cried, and caused a flood

In her beautiful voice if she'd ordain
For her I would be dying again and again

The fire that's hidden within my breast
The fire of sun it can easily contest

Having given my heart, I'm the kind of guy
Who'd be crying and crying if he didn't die

And though I've a wonderful temperament
For moaning and groaning I've a natural bent

And there are though, GHALIB, poets galore
They say I'm the sweetest troubadour

41

Laazim tha keh daeko mera rasta koie din aur

O tell me why didn't you wait for me
And why from me did you have to flee?

Oh, why so soon did you go away
And why by your side you wouldn't let me stay?

You were hardly here when you went away
But what was the hurry; why didn't you stay?

I know in Heaven you're going to dwell
But why did you leave me here in this hell?

But he was so young, my Aarif, O fate
For a few more years O why couldn't you wait?

My nights are dark without his moon
O how could you take him away so soon?

Oh, he was my blood, my life breath
Why didn't you spare him, O Angel of Death?

His beautiful children you could let him enjoy
And the joy of his wife you didn't have to destroy

The problems of life he didn't have to evade
Why, a little bit longer he could have stayed

This life, O GHALIB, without him I hate
How long for my death will I have to wait?

42

Na gul e naghma houn na perda e saaz

It's surely not music, O can't you tell
For to me it sounds like a tolling bell

She's always arranging her curly hair
And here, my hair I'm ready to tear

The boasting is only for a simpleton
With my pain and sorrow I've been overrun

Oh, I'm a bird who's made to soar
But I'm in love with my predator

And she has her ego; she has her pride
But my love is also very dignified

Oh, I'm a victim of her long eyelashes
With them my heart oh, how she slashes

And about her beauty I rave and rave
For she is my queen, and I'm her slave

Oh, when she flirts, she looks like a rose
And when she's cruel, it seems like a pose

And when her lovers she comes to meet
They fall on the ground, and kiss her feet

And, GHALIB, I love the beautiful girls
For to me they're like the gems and pearls

43
Muzhda aey zoaq e aseeri keh nazar aa'ta hay

Rejoice, O prey, the huntress is here
She's coming to get you with all her gear

You're a bird of prey but you're lovelorn
So your rose is coming carrying the thorn

Oh, I was so sick I could not see
When she came to express her sympathy

I wish she would come and take my life
And bring with her the sharpest knife

I can't get away; it's no use tryin'
For she is more dangerous than a hungry lion

But when in the garden she came and sat
The flowers leapt up and went to her hat

So, GHALIB, you know, I'll soon be dead
For against her wall I'm banging my head

44

Aah ko chaahiay ik umr asar honay tak

The wishes take ages to materialize
And I'll not live to win the prize

O when it begins, it's only a dot
But to become a pearl it takes a lot

Oh, love wants patience and the wish has none
And this waiting and waiting, well, it's no fun

I know my darling, she will not delay
But what if she comes and I'm on my way

Oh, I'm like dew and she is like sun
When I'll see her face, I'll be undone

And life is short and the time flies
And we're dead and gone before we realize

And, GHALIB, for sorrow there's no cure
So whatever comes I'll have to endure

45
Wo firaaq aur wo wisaal kahaan

The meetings and partings are there no more
O whatever happened to the days of yore?

What happened to yearning, and where is desire
And where're the people who beauty admire?

Those rosy cheeks why the people forgot
And where are the lovers of the beauty spot?

The mention of love only brings up a yawn
And the notion of beauty is all but gone

And whatever happened to the tears of blood?
They used to rain, oh, they used to flood

On love and beauty why nobody gambles?
Why the betting places are all in shambles?

How the love on people has lost its clout
Now everyday woes they all worry about

In my problems, GHALIB, I'm also mired
Oh, I feel so weak; I feel so tired

46

Ki wafa hum say toe ghair is ko jafa kehtay haen

Don't listen to my rival; be kind to me
For goodness in anyone he just cannot see

I have come to tell you my pain and sorrow
O please don't tell me to come back tomorrow

You know, my love, I'm a traditional guy
And to drown my sorrow in the wine I try

You can make me cry to your heart's content
But I'm sure one day you're going to relent

Oh, I must be a fool who's totally misled
For why I worship is above my head

O look from where I've come to meet
So please take pity on my blistered feet

And it's not love and it's not desire
What I have in my heart is a blazing fire

They say you're proud, and it may be true
But you're my goddess, and I worship you

And GHALIB tells me when I will die
Everyone will say he was quite a guy

47

Aabroo kya khaak us gul ki keh gulshan maen naheen

When not in the garden, a flower is lost
O don't you pluck it; just think of the cost

Your tears, O lover, you need not dread
The blood in your heart is meant to be shed

You're a speck of dirt that's seen by none
Unless you shine in the beam of the sun

The dungeon of sorrow is deadly and dark
Of hope in it there's not even a spark

Oh, what's a lover if he does not yearn?
And what's a fire if it does not burn?

Your wounded heart, O leave it alone
It's there to bleed and not to be sewn

When a hapless lover does go to his grave
For a glimpse of his flower he still does crave

And remains he always true to his creed
And his wounded heart does bleed and bleed

And a lover doesn't care what anyone thinks
He goes to the bar, and drinks and drinks

And even when he grows very weak and old
He does not bend, and he does not fold

And, GHALIB, in desert when he goes to roam
He finds a home away from his home

48
Hum say khhul jaao ba waqt e maiparasti aek din

While we are drinking, let's sit and neck
Let us hug and smooch, yes, what the heck?

This world of ours is but an illusion
And surely in this there's no confusion

I always borrowed money in order to drink
Until in poverty I started to sink

In our crazy world nobody can be glad
So if I'm sad, it's not that bad

But I'm very sorry for the hullaballoo
For GHALIB says I was being fresh with you

49

Hum per jafa say tark e wafa ka gumaan naheen

My love and sincerity she cannot doubt
Then why's she so cruel, and what's it about?

And though she'll never say it to me
I think she likes me to a certain degree

Sometimes I feel she's not so unkind
So when she is callous, I do not mind

And although it sounds all very absurd
I love and cherish every unkind word

And though her cruelty is certainly wrong
And though I'm not patient and not so strong

And though it may sound harsh and severe
Every word that she utters I love to hear

And whether she uses a dagger or a dart
I wish she would come and wound my heart

Oh, what's a heart if it doesn't have desire?
And what's a sigh if it doesn't have fire?

And I do not mind burning my home
I'll go to the desert and there I'll roam

Oh, it's in my blood, in my very core
My gorgeous idol I was born to adore

And me when my beautiful idol inspires
The verses I write even Gabriel admires

So, GHALIB, if she'd let me kiss her feet
I'll gladly give my life for such a treat

50
Manay e dashtnawardi koie tadbeer naheen

In search of his love a lover must roam
His prison is desert and also his home

To win his beloved if he does aspire
He has to follow his urge and desire

The pang of love is a lover's reward
It stabs his heart like a double sword

With his pain and sorrow he has to cope
And even after that there's little hope

His wounds he savors more and more
And before it can heal, he picks his sore

But he can be also curt and bold
Whenever he gains a little foothold

And though, GHALIB, as a poet he may be good
He defers to Meer as a poet should

51
Jahaan taera naqsh e qadam daekhtay haen

Your footsteps, darling, wherever they see
That they'll lead to Heaven they all agree

And whenever they see the mole on your cheek
They think their prospects are all too bleak

And your shapely figure, oh, it's so pretty
There're riots and riots all over the city

When your face in the glass you see and admire
You set the hearts of your lovers on fire

So with the hearts aflame, and the minds blown
They cry all night, and moan, and groan

Then, GHALIB, as beggars they roam in the city
In the hope on them people will take pity

52

Milti hay khoo e yaar say naar iltahaab maen

Oh, when she's angry, she gives me hell
But when she scolds, in heaven dwell

I have lived too long, some people say
But they count the time when she's away

She came in my dream and said she'll visit
Since then I haven't slept, not even a bit

When I send her a letter, I know the reply
So I do not wait, and again I try

But when she serves, it tastes divine
I think she mixes something in the wine

And about my rival I do not worry
For favor from her he cannot curry

But he surely knows to pussyfoot
And doubt in her mind he can easily put

And when she comes, being an amateur
I forget to tell her that I'll die for her

Then she gets upset, and wears a veil
And I moan, and groan, and cry, and wail

And then she pouts, and does not stir
And ignores completely my feelings for her

So my moaning and groaning are of no use
And the effect desired they do not produce

Now magic and voodoo I think I'll try
They say on them you can surely rely

And my drinking, GHALIB, I try to fight
But I can't resist it on a moonlit night

53
Kal kay liay ker aaj na khissat sharaab maen

O don't be stingy with the cup of wine
For your Heavenly vat has plenty of wine

Yes, we're all topers; we drink very hard
Even angels for us have a lot of regard

At the sound of music we go in a trance
We hear from God and dance and dance

We don't know the goal; and without a course
Our life is like a runaway horse

And what are we, we do not know
We doubt each other, whether friend or foe

Oh, we're the observers, and we're the observed
We see our backs, our sights are curved

There's nothing in the ocean; it's only an illusion
These waves and storms are a source of confusion

The overt and the hidden are one and the same
What's hidden in the candle comes out as a flame

When beauty acquires a form female
A mirror it keeps behind the veil

We think we're awake, or so it may seem
But still we're dreaming while awake in a dream

And, GHALIB, to you it may sound rather odd
But in Ali I see the image of God

54

Hairaan houn dil ko rooun keh peetoun jigger ko maen

I've wailed and cried as much as I could
Now hire a mourner, I think, I should

Everyone I ask, O where should I go?
But the address of her house I'll never show

I go to the house of my terrible foe
For there, I'm certain, she loves to go

When her waist is already beyond compare
A corset, I don't know, why she has to wear?

For her I've destroyed my beautiful place
But still she thinks I'm low and base

Oh, I follow every person who is on the go
But where am I going I do not know

And though idol-worship I'm not for
My beautiful idol I simply adore

I'm lost to the world, oh, I'm in a trance
I've lost my beloved; I don't have a chance

And though I'm doing whatever I can
There's no one who cares for an able man

But, GHALIB, there's one thing I surely need
I want to see Ali on his white steed

55

Zikr maera ba badi bhee usay manzoor naheen

No, she wouldn't hear anything about me
So let him say what he wants, my enemy

She said in the park she'll take a walk
But about me killing she wouldn't even talk

When I said, "In Heaven you'll sit on my knee"
She said, "I'm no houri; don't talk to me"

As long as she's mine, whether she's fair
Or cruel and callous, I do not care

Oh, the woes of my love have made me weak
I'm sick and tired; my future is bleak

But I'm a toper with a magical bowl
In it I can find the secret of my soul

To her waist this world I can easily compare
O yes, it's there, but it's also not there

But I don't agree with the mystical notion
I may be a drop but I'm not the ocean

But, GHALIB, of poetry I may be the king
When compared to Zahoori I'm just nothing

56

Naala juz husn e talab aey sitameejaad naheen

O if I'm crying, it's not to complain
She doesn't have to be nice; there's nothing to explain

To be a Romeo, it is not my aim
And if I love her, it's not for fame

I like the space in which to roam
Otherwise the desert is just like home

The experience of living is a teacher great
You become an expert when you graduate

Of the pangs of love I'm going to die
I'm so very weak, I can't even cry

And when in the garden there's no breeze
The tulips and roses lose luster and ease

And when the gardener plucks a rose
He gives the birds a lot of woes

Her mouth with a rosebud you can compare
It is so small, it's hardly there

Her street is just like the paradise
It's a lot more busy but just as nice

Oh, I feel like an alien in this dreadful city
There's no one here, GHALIB, who has any pity

57
Naheen keh mujh ko qayaamat ka aateqaad naheen

The night of parting has nothing but torment
It's just as trying as the Day of Judgment

I like to drink on a fine day
But on a moonlit night I also may

When I go to see her, she never says hi
And when I leave, there's no good-bye

And when I'm away, she always says why
He's not here, that troublesome guy?

She'd let me drink on a festive occasion
But the rest of the time she needs persuasion

Oh, there's no joy; I've only pain
But this is my fate; I cannot complain

And, GHALIB, a promise she'll never make
Unless this promise she intends to break

58
Teray tosan ko saba baandhtay haen

I want the breeze to blow and blow
And spread my word as I crow and crow

My sighing and crying are of no use
No feelings of pity can they induce

Oh, life is short and the time flies
And a little bit of rest oh, how it denies

A life of pain is difficult to bear
There's moaning, and groaning, and a lot of despair

The flowers are drunk with color and bloom
Look, how they adorn themselves and groom

O yourself in moaning do not involve
The problems of life it cannot solve

The stragglers, look, how they operate
They nurse their blisters and decorate

And the beauties, GHALIB, they are so cool
Look, how their lovers they lure and fool

59

Da'im perha hua teray der per naheen houn maen

Forever I will not knock at her door
And I won't be always a mat on her floor

Oh, everyone gives me a run around
I go round and round, like a merry-go-round

To me it's a puzzle and a mystery
But everyone, it seems, is after me

I do not know why I'm in this hell
I'm only a sinner, not an infidel

They think I'm worthless because I'm old
Though I'm not a gem; I'm not gold

But I think with the sun I am at par
And I'm as high as any star

And still she would not come out to greet
And wouldn't even let me kiss her feet

But, GHALIB, in spite of everything
I'm so very grateful to our generous king

60

Sub kahaan kuchh laala o gul maen numaayaan ho gaien

As beautiful flowers come out they must
The lovely women that lie in the dust

Oh, how I remember the fun we've had
Now it's all gone and it's so sad

The beauties in the day are out of sight
But like the stars they're naked at night

Though Jacob from Joseph did not hear
He cried and cried; was his pain so severe

And Potiphar's wife was not so glad
When she saw that girls about Joseph were mad

When blood, in her absence, my eyes shed
They change my cheeks from pale to red

I'll take my revenge in heaven, I swear
If these beauties become the houris there

And I also think it is not very fair
On my rivals arm when she spreads her hair

My moaning and groaning when to the park I bring
The birds, when they hear me, start to sing

Her long eyelashes are like the darts
The strike, they jab, they go through the hearts

My fiery sighs when I try to suppress
My chest explodes, and it becomes a mess

I can take her abuse but how I hate
When her awful doorman I've to adulate

But when a drink she offers, I come alive
The wine to me does a lot to revive

For the rites of religion I do not care
Though belief and faith, I think, are fair

Yes, when it's too painful, it seems quite breezy
And when it's too hard, it becomes rather easy

But, GHALIB, if she lets me cry and cry
The world might drown, and it might die

61

Deewaangi say doash pay zinnaar bhee naheen

I'm totally mad; my clothes are torn
Oh, I'm so exhausted, so tired, so worn

With my beautiful gal I would love to be
But me she dazzles, and I cannot see

Oh, love is a slope that's very, very greasy
And it may look easy but it isn't so easy

A life without love is not really life
Though love has plenty of pain and strife

These crazy ideas in my head I dread
I should go to a wall and smash my head

Away from my rivals a place I seek
My love has made me so frail and weak

Oh, I'm her captive; I'm her prey
To me some attention I wish she'd pay

Her long eyelashes are daggers and knives
When stabbed by them, no heart survives

And when she's angry, her lovers take flight
She has no sword but she can really fight

So, GHALIB, by now it should be quite plain
I may not be crazy but neither am I sane

62
Naheen hay zakhm koie bakhiay kay derkhur meray tan maen

My gaping wounds O please don't sew
And my blood in tears, just let it flow

My house is ruined; there's nothing to see
My flooding tears are up to my knee

My blood is dripping from all my slashes
For I'm a victim of her long eyelashes

My life is bleak; my house is dark
Of light in them you can't see a spark

And whenever they see my insanity
My friends rebuke and laugh at me

And when she herself in the mirror admires
Oh, how it yearns for her and desires

I don't know whether I'm good or bad
But fate is against me, and it's so sad

My heart is mad; I'm totally insane
And on my blood my love is a drain

But her captive, GHALIB, I still remain
Around my neck her arms are a chain

63
Mazay jahaan kay apni nazar maen khaak naheen

O there's no pleasure; O there's no fun
Those yearnings and cravings O there're none

My wings have been clipped; I've lost my flair
I feel like the dust that's floating in the air

Rejoice, O heart, go beat the drum
My beautiful gal is about to come

My sighing and crying are of no use
No pity, no mercy can they induce

When the topers go to the bar and drink
Of beautiful girls they sit there and think

Everything in my heart my love has killed
It's so very desolate, you cannot rebuild

But, GHALIB, to me what's most worrisome
How silly and frivolous my poetry has become

64

Dil hi toe hay na sang o khisht, dard say bhar na aa'ay kuin

I'm made of flesh and not of stone
So hurt me not, and I'll not moan

It's neither a temple nor a retreat
Don't drive me out; it's only a street

Your coming in public O do not curtail
And you're so dazzling you don't need a veil

Your lash is a dagger and glance a dart
So it's hard to face you, my sweetheart

An eternal bliss only death can claim
For life and sorrow are one and the same

In grace and beauty when you are the best
Your hapless lovers then why do you test?

With me so reserved, and you so proud
No wonder our meeting fate hasn't allowed

And if you're not faithful and not sincere
Why do they all come to see you here?

And the truth is for GHALIB people don't care
And nothing stops when he is not there

65

Ghuncha e nashagufta ko dour say met dikha keh yuin

She shows me her lipstick from so very far
When I'd rather kiss her lips the way they are

Oh, the way she smiles and the way she winks
And her beautiful eyes the way she blinks

But with my foe when she sits and drinks
She looks like a rose; he simply stinks

And when with my rival she spends the night
She blows me up with the dynamite

But comes she when to take the stock
I get tongue-tied, and just can't talk

To leave my foe when I asked her once
She asked me to leave, and I felt like a dunce

It wasn't very smart, and I paid the cost
I was completely blown; I was totally lost

So all night long I was up on my feet
And up and down I was going in her street

To have my gal I yearn and crave
I'm anxious and restive like a tidal wave

But my verses in Urdu when, GHALIB, she reads
They're better than in Persian she simply concedes

66
Waarasta is say haen keh mohabbat hi kuin na ho

If our feelings of love we cannot restore
You're welcome to hate me but please don't ignore

I'm weak, and old, and beyond repair
And your love is a burden very hard to bear

When you mention my foe, it gives me pain
Even when I know you're trying to complain

When for every ailment there is a cure
Why the pangs of love do we've to endure?

Oh, I've been crippled; I've been maimed
And yes, I'm helpless, but I'm not ashamed

I'm always absorbed in thoughts my own
So I'm never lonely when I'm alone

And I may be lame but I'm not tame
For a lack of courage is to me a shame

In the lack of concern there may be a danger
Too much autonomy can make you a stranger

From pain and sorrow I can't get away
No matter how much I plead and pray

And you may ignore me, or you may deplore
But your GHALIB will never leave your door

67

Qafas maen houn, ger achha bhee
na jaanaen maeray shavan ko

Sitting in a cage while I cry and cry
Around me the birds all sing and fly

O tell my rival to give me a break
His raving about her I just can't take

When sewing my wounds even the surgeons cry
But she does not care even if I die

I don't like my hands when out of despair
They rip my clothes, and they tear my hair

And riding her horse oh, how she hovers
And one by one how she kills her lovers

And chains when they cast for my wounded feet
The heart of iron does melt with the heat

And during the drought when I pray for rain
I'm struck by lightning and a hurricane

O if you are consistent in faith and creed
God will reward you for it indeed

I do not mind my blood being shed
In front of her sword I bow my head

And if I'm robbed in broad day light
I feel so relieved I sleep all night

And if with me things do get worse
In writing my verses I completely immerse

And even then badly if I need something
I then go, GHALIB, and see my king

68
Waan pounhach ker jo ghash aata pay e hum hay hum ko

To kiss her feet whenever I try
She pulls them back, and says - O my!

To her my heart is always loyal
But for me this love is full of turmoil

This yoke of love is anything but fun
I cannot stay, and I cannot run

Her beguiling look is hard to survive
But her charming glance, it can also revive

And it's hard to take the dreadful wail
Of a lonely lovesick nightingale

When I asked one day if she likes me dead
She swore by my life she wants my head

She wants not only my heart to bleed
But also my blood in my tears indeed

She makes a promise and makes me wait
But my crying for her she can't tolerate

And when I travelled to Lucknaow
She said, "It's not the place for you

"For peace to you it cannot bestow
To Mecca or Najaf you ought to go"

So, GHALIB, I want to be in a city
Where there's mercy, and love, and pity

69
Tum jaano tum ko ghair say jo rasm o raah ho

Your seeing my rival I do not mind
If to me you're also a little more kind

On the Judgment Day you'll be in the dock
For you saw my rival giving me the sock

Is it also as cruel, my love, as you are?
For you're so like Venus, the morning star

And how come, darling, I always fail
When my rival has access behind the veil

And if in the saloon I can't get the wine
I might as well go and sit in a shrine

Of the wonders of Heaven I'm very aware
But I certainly hope I'll find you there

For me, says GHALIB, no one does care
But they pray our sovereign is always there

70

Gaie wo baat keh ho guftogoo toe kuinker ho

It's hard for me to talk to you
For you never listen even when I do

Of meeting you, darling, there's not a chance
I just can't think of any circumstance

With my regard for you I cannot insist
And you being coy, you always resist

Someone like you is very hard to woo
And I do not know how the others do

When looking in the mirror, you get upset
For a siren like you is to you a threat

I feel so gloomy I see no light
And even my day is dark as night

With your disdain I cannot cope
It's so discouraging, I have no hope

And even when you write me a nice note
For me it's never an antidote

If one of your glances I manage to grab
Your long eyelashes, oh, how they stab

But as king to your GHALIB has said so well
Life without a gal is a veritable hell

71

Kisi ko day kay dil koie nawasanj e fughaan kuin ho

You have given your heart, O why do you cry?
There's nothing you can do, so don't even try

You know it's her nature; you can easily see
Don't ask her why is she always angry?

Your pain and sorrow if he can't comprehend
He's no help though he may be a friend

And if with your gal you can't get ahead
Against her door don't bang your head

You know, you're a captive; you're in a cage
From your home and garden you should disengage

O you're in love, but it is not right
She's always in your heart but never in sight

In her heart affection you cannot infuse
This pulling and pushing is of no use

So don't even try; it can never be
When fate is also your enemy

And when she knows you'll never do
Why is she always testing you?

Oh, she is a siren; she is a flirt
And she treats you like a speck of dirt

And you'll end up causing a lot of stir
It's no use, GHALIB, your taunting her

72
Masjid kay zaer e saaya kharaabaat chahiay

From the mosque to the tavern it's not very far
In the eyes of a lover they're both on a par

I know she's in love with another man
But be nice to this lover she also can

Oh, my heart is full of a million desires
But help from luck it also requires

Well, I became a painter because of her
But she thinks I am only an amateur

For the sake of pleasure I do not drink
I need a trance in which to sink

To see the flowers I go to the park
Of youth in them I find the mark

And face I Mecca when I go to pray
And near the vat in the bar I stay

And in the pub they think that I'm odd
Because when there I get drunk with God

So quietly, GHALIB, you can achieve a lot
And say an awful lot when speak you not

73

Bisaat e ijz maen tha aek dil, yak qatra khoon wo bhee

There's not much blood in my poor little heart
From much more of it I simply can't part

Oh, she has given me a lot of pain
No more will I take it; it's totally insane

Sometimes I say I would like to die
But on a wish like this I cannot rely

And my moaning and groaning are of no use
My intense pain they cannot reduce

In her cruelty she takes a lot of pride
And I do not mind; I take it in stride

Any good from my fate I do not expect
And whatever it gives, I cannot reject

But the pain of her absence is my biggest bane
And about it, GHALIB, I've a right to complain

74
Gham e dunya say ger paaie bhee fursat ser uthhanay ki

Some respite when I get from sorrow and pain
Her memory comes back to haunt me again

It's no use sending her a nice note
She'll burn it, or throw it somewhere remote

It's easier to hide in your clothes the fire
Than to hide in your heart a burning desire

When she goes in the street to take a walk
Of her wounded lovers she takes the stock

She has come to stay I like to believe
But she comes to my place only to leave

It's easier for me to live with her pride
Than my everyday woes to take in stride

And when you're good and others are bad
It makes you feel, GHALIB, so very sad

75
Kya tang hum sitamzadagaan ka jahaan hay

The world of a lover is all too wide
And a million skies it can hold inside

The realm of beauty is without any bound
And it's the love that makes the world go round

And what may look like the ruby wine
Are my tears of blood in the cup of mine

A loving heart she does not trust
Instead she likes one full of lust

She says my rival she did not kiss
And she wants me to believe a thing like this

And he knows love if anybody can
The august emperor of Hindustan

In love my faith is total and blind
In sorrow my reason of being I find

And even though, GHALIB, she is unkind
The pain she gives I do not mind

76
Dard say maeray hay tujh ko baiqaraari, haay, haay

She now worries about my grief and pain
But how could it happen, I cannot explain?

But if she's so bothered by my agony
She shouldn't have come to comfort me

On me her kindness she shouldn't confer
For it seems my friendship is not good for her

She has vowed to spend her life with me
But in life there is no guarantee

I'm thoroughly fed up with this life of mine
So her life with mine she should not entwine

To give up vanity O why did she decide?
And whatever happened to her famous pride?

But clues to her feelings she does not give
Oh, why has she become so secretive?

The pangs of love, O where did they go?
No high, no low; no ebb, no flow

What happened to her dagger, it's hard to know?
And where is her arrow, and where is her bow?

When it's rainy and dark and no moonlight
How the lovers can count the stars at night?

And for a lover it just cannot be
No message to hear, no beauty to see

So, GHALIB, these things you cannot fix
For love and sanity just do not mix

77
Sergashtagi maen aalam e hasti say yaas hay

The reality of being is greatly in doubt
It's hard to know what it's all about

For my poor little heart she does not care
As long as she knows it's not going anywhere

For the sake of my gal, I love my pain
And grateful to her I'll always remain

The pride in her beauty has made her haughty
She can also be nice, though a little bit naughty

I like to drink in a moonlit night
And I feel better when things aren't right

And, GHALIB, it's nice that someone does care
The desert feels lonely when I'm not there

78
Ger khaamashi say faaida ikhfa e haal hay

Oh, talking to the people I'd like to quit
For me they cannot understand a bit

The urge to talk cannot be overcome
Though I try to pretend I'm deaf and dumb

I believe whatever will be, will be
So question I cannot whatever I see

And careless and proud though she may be
I don't think she is my enemy

The shroud of Kaaba is because of Ali
And millions of people around it rally

My grief is huge, and the world is small
They create an ocean where my tears fall

And, GHALIB my friend, it's my conclusion
That this world of ours is just an illusion

79

Aek ja herf e wafa likhha so wo bhee mit gaya

The word sincerity I think you wrote
Then why was it rubbed off from your note?

I cannot believe, when I'm breathing fire
That it is not burning my body entire

All things make noise when you roast them or fry
But I always stay silent; I don't even cry

The presence of God makes the earth feel drunk
And to the moon and stars gives all their spunk

O when with my life I'm in such despair
To call you my life it doesn't seem fair

And in my letter I have put my eyes
So when you read, they say – surprise, surprise!

80
Ishq mujh ko naheen wehshat hi sahi

I'm totally insane, and I'm to blame
But let my madness become your fame

O please don't end our relationship
This budding flower oh, do not nip

And if with me you don't want to be seen
Then let me use a go-between

Be a casual friend if you possibly can
I know you're in love in another man

I know, my darling, you're not perfect
So mind I will not a little neglect

Oh, life is short and the time flies
So on what I have, let me capitalize

I don't mind troubles; I don't mind woes
For your sake, my love, I'll put up with foes

I'm not in a hurry; I'll patiently wait
And learn to live with my cruel fate

I promise to you I'll not be upset
And take from you whatever I get

And GHALIB tells me that I should not pout
And if I can't have you, I should do without

81
Us buzm maen mujhay naheen banti haya kiay

Oh, how in her salon, where I'm normally shy
She sends me the signals by winking her eye

Her doorman is a fellow I simply abhor
So I go like a beggar and knock at her door

And the barman in the pub is truly a clown
To purchase a drink I've to pawn my gown

So a short life is more than enough for me
And I don't want to live till eternity

And sometimes I ask the dust, "O you
With all those beauties what did you do?"

My terrible rivals oh, how I despise
I put up with all their slanders and lies

She'd never ever kiss me, but my rival to spite
She kissed me once in a moonlit night

And sometimes I am amazed to find
That she simply forgets to be unkind

But, GHALIB, when I go to her in tears
I don't know what I say and what she hears?

82

Daekhna qismat keh aap apnay pay rashk aa jaay hay

Of anyone who sees her I'm jealous outright
And I also even envy my own eyesight

The maid of the bar is quite a lass
Her pungent wine does melt my glass

She is also bashful and rather coy
But a little seduction she seems to enjoy

My passion demands that I cry and cry
But I find it difficult to satisfy

But when she hears it, she say, O my!
May God protect her from the evil eye

And when I'm lost, people do infer
That I'm madly, madly in love with her

And when she invites me to her salon
She makes me feel I'm only a pawn

And by her manners infer I can
That she's in love with another man

And when her picture I want to draw
She becomes very pale and filled with awe

But, GHALIB, I am my biggest enemy
Even my shadow's running away from me

83
Saadgi per us ki mer jaanay ki hasrat dil maen hay

Oh, she is so simple, when she takes my life
She wants to kill me with a dagger or a knife

On her keen perception I'm totally hung
For what I'm thinking is on her tongue

And even though bad, when they talk about me
I feel as proud as I possibly can be

I don't mind failing; I'm that kind of a guy
Who feels very happy whenever he can try

But I'm so tired, I do not care
Whether I stay or go somewhere

My heart is on fire; it is like hell
And she's a bombshell, that beautiful belle

And, GHALIB, I'm burning with a mad desire
And it is consuming my being entire

84

Dil say teri nigaah jigger tak utar gaie

Her eyes have captured my heart and soul
And now they are in complete control

My chest is rent; it is open wide
My wounded heart now I cannot hide

Last night I drank a lot of wine
But now it's time to rise and shine

My nest is ruined; I have lost my things
I'm now a bird without the wings

Look how she swings, and how she rocks
And nobody walks the way she walks

Now everyone calls himself a lover
But faced with trouble, he takes the cover

And when he sees her gorgeous face
He's totally dazzled by her beauty and grace

And when she leaves him for someone else
His utter destruction she quickly spells

And, GHALIB, like me he's a victim of time
Which is slowly draining away his prime

85
Taskeen ko hum na roaen jo zoaq e nazer milay

If I could have her, I wouldn't cry
I pray she's my houri after I die

But I could become the greatest lover
If free from my terrible troubles I were

And me with her address if she could provide
I wouldn't be needing anymore a guide

The way he behaves, you can easily infer
That my courier is also in love with her

O bury me not in her neighborhood
For find her home that way they would

O maid of the bar, you're so divine
Do quench my thirst, and give me some wine

And, GHALIB, if they see a lover with passion
Please tell her neighbors to show compassion

86
Koie din ger zindagaani aur hay

If a little bit longer I could be around
I'd leave this world with a mark profound

Oh, the fire of hell cannot be so hot
As the blaze of love in my heart I've got

Oh, many a times I have seen her mad
But so much fury she has never had

And when her letter the courier brought
I wish I hadn't asked him what she thought

The stars in heaven are all against me
And the fate is also my enemy

And, GHALIB, sorrow I can't have more
Now the Angel of Death I'm waiting for

87
Koie ummeed ber naheen aati

For a man like me there is no hope
To find my way I grope and grope

And all night long I weep and weep
It becomes so bad, I can hardly sleep

Oh, there was a time when I could smile
Now I don't do it even once in a while

The rewards of piety I certainly know
But to the preacher I say - no thank you, no

I've become so quiet, I can hardly talk
And when they speak, I simply gawk

But then I go to the other extreme
And if they don't listen, I yell and scream

If my burning heart they cannot see
They can surely see my agony

And when my feelings I totally exhaust
I begin to feel I am completely lost

And then I want to cry and cry
And feel so sick that I want to die

And what should I do when I'm feeling low?
To Mecca, says GHALIB, I ought to go

88
Dil e naadaan tujhay hua kya hay

O my foolish heart, what's wrong with you?
Why are you always feeling so blue?

Oh, I'm so eager and she's so cold
But that's her nature I have been told

I am not mute; I do have a tongue
Why doesn't she ask me why am I hung?

Oh, in Your being I don't have a doubt
But tell me, O God, what's it all about?

Why do we have these beautiful girls?
And what are the brows and the raven curls?

And why do they have such charming eyes?
And why do they enchant and mesmerize?

And what're the clouds, and what's the breeze?
And why are there flowers, bushes, and trees?

And why do the lovers hold them so dear
The girls who're faithless and insincere?

For my beautiful gal I yearn and crave
Though I'm a beggar and a lowly slave

And I'll not falter; I'll not demur
If she needs my life, I'll give it for her

And, GHALIB, I wonder what's wrong with me?
And why doesn't she take me when I'm for free?

89

Kehtay toe ho tum sab keh but e ghaaliamoo aa'ay

My beautiful gal is a debonair
And everyone loves her fragrant hair

She came as lightening; went out as flame
Who knows where she went, and whence she came?

To have my gal I'll pay any cost
For if I don't find her, I'll be totally lost

Even going to Mecca I will not mind
For I will seek her until I find

My time is up; I'm about to die
I wish she'd come to say good-bye

When the angels quiz me after my death
I hope they won't test for liquor my breath

But I'll welcome any kind of creature
Whether it's a hangman, a priest, or a preacher

But I feel so helpless I cry and cry
And even on my friends I cannot rely

For to her salon even when they go
How to help me, GHALIB, they do not know

90
Phir kuchh ik dil ko baiqaraari hay

My heart is restless it's very, very skittish
To be stabbed and wounded it can only wish

My heart and eyes are my real foes
Their yearning and craving cause all my woes

And behind the curtain when she tries to hide
My eyes want to go and look inside

And when in the park she takes a stroll
My silly little heart gets out of control

To contain my sorrow I try and try
And when I fail, I moan and cry

Like a bird without flower I wail and wail
And dig my wounds with my fingernail

Oh, I cannot explain; I can't tell you why?
But at her feet I would like to die

So she is my life, my only goal
And love her I do with my heart and soul

And whether it is fair or not so fair
We're all the prisoners of her curly hair

The rules she makes you cannot repeal
And to no other jury can you appeal

Your sin of loving her she'll not condone
She'll make you cry, and moan, and groan

You can bring your friends to testify
But you'll be ordered to forever cry

For the rest of your life you'll have the blues
And she'll surely win and you're bound to lose

And, GHALIB, forever she'll put you in a trance
And on her tune she'll make you dance

91
Baiaatadaalion say subuk sub maen hum huway

In immoderation those who believe
The more they desire, the less they receive

Too close to home there was her snare
I could not escape; I didn't have a prayer

Oh, it's not so very difficult to guess
That everything ends in nothingness

And you may like it or you may not
But pain and sorrow are a lover's lot

And if you can escape the lover's curse
There're a lot of pains that are even worse

But in the end you'll have to concede
That a lover's lot is to bleed and bleed

And if your girl is cruel and tart
You can easily write off your poor little heart

But then there're people who only lust
And, unlike lovers, they don't go bust

And then there are those you can't satisfy
They are born to always cry and cry

And, GHALIB, you know me from cover to cover
I'm a man who was born to be a lover

92

Zulmatkaday maen maeray shab e gham ka joash hay

My house is as dark as the darkest night
Only a candle is there and it's silent quite

There's nothing to hear and nothing to see
And it's all as quiet as it can be

Oh, after she drinks, she's not very shy
And to her reserve she says good-bye

And around her neck when pearls she wears
Her jeweler can't talk; he simply stares

She makes them drunk, your heart and soul
And on your mind you lose control

So I say to you who are new to this
And the good things in life if you don't want to miss

That before you plunge, you ought to see
And learn from a lover who's old like me

These beautiful girls are a different breed
And for the maid of the bar you can lose your creed

When you enter the bar during night hours
It looks like a garden all full of flowers

When the music plays and the beauties dance
It's so hypnotic you can go in a trance

But early in the morning it's the other extreme
And you feel as if it was only a dream

And feeling the night's parting pains
Only a weeping candle there remains

Now, GHALIB, I only hear a hum
And don't know from where these ideas come

93
Aa keh meri jaan ko qaraar naheen hay

O come and put my heart at ease
And don't make me wait forever please

The wine in Heaven, it may be divine
But if you can't get drunk, why drink the wine?

In her salon she doesn't want me to cry
But how do I keep my eyes dry?

She always says I get her upset
But that she's sensitive, I always forget

And when I see the flowers in the spring
They make me forget about everything

To take my life she has promised to come
But before she comes, I'm going to succumb

And, GHALIB, she says she'll drink with me
But to change her mind she's absolutely free

94

Jis bazm maen too naaz say guftaar maen aaway

Oh, in her salon when she starts to talk
To pick up the pearls around her they flock

And when in the park she takes a walk
All the cypress trees, they start to rock

But no one cares for the lovers' tears
Unless the blood in their eyes appears

And nobody cares if they do not complain
Of the wounds of love, and pangs, and pain

When she looks at it, her charming eyes
They enchant the mirror and mesmerize

And the thorns get dried in the desert heat
If she doesn't feed them on her lovers' feet

But when she binds on her lovers the spell
Oh, how they love her, their infidel

But the beautiful girls do love the gold
Like tulips and roses they are bought and sold

And the lovers watch with great despair
And rip their clothes and tear their hair

Their breaths have fire; their hearts have pain
But they hide their wounds, and do not complain

And though they may sound quite absurd
But, GHALIB, it has meaning, their every word

95
Husn e meh gercheh ba hungaam e kamal achha hay

Yes, the moon looks lovely when it is full
But she's always gorgeous and beautiful

She takes his heart because it's free
But leaves her lover in much agony

His earthen cup, oh, it's a disgrace
But unlike Jum's, it's easy to replace

So if you can help it, don't strip his mask
And give this beggar before he can ask

He feels so happy when he sees his belle
But she thinks her patient is doing very well

Maybe he'll be lucky; she won't be severe
For a Brahman says it'll be a good year

And in order to have his lovely Juliet
A Romeo can use any help he can get

And it's best for a lover to have the notion
That he is drop and his love is an ocean

And may God bless our wonderful king
And may his garden always have spring

And, GHALIB, a person should try to be nice
And should not worry about going to paradise

96

Na hui ger meray mernay say tasalli na sahi

When I died, she said that I wasn't tough
And that she could not test me enough

I do not regret that I finally died
But I'm sorry she wasn't there by my side

I can have the wine, though I despair
When the maid of the bar I can't find there

The desert is happy when lovers are there
But whether they're happy it does not care

And as long as there is a lot of fanfare
Whether it's wedding or funeral it does not care

I give to my verses whatever I've got
And don't care if they're popular or not

And, GHALIB, I know you won't agree
But with the beautiful girls I like to be

97
Shikway kay naam say baimehr khafa hota hay

Oh, she's not very happy when I complain
But if I don't, she prods me again and again

But I like to talk without any doubt
You just have to ask me; I'll blurt it out

And whenever I am a little bit jealous
She becomes very spiteful, cruel, and callous

But this is not the end of the cruelty
My fate is also my great enemy

But I so much like a wounded heart
And if she misses, I return her the dart

Oh, whatever I want, the opposite I get
So I think on the opposite I should always bet

They used to pity me when I would cry
But now on my tears I cannot rely

But my poet's pen still has the power
And above all the poets of the court I tower

Our king who rules the earth and the sky
And on whose generosity we can always rely

He has in his army the best of men
And the amount of his wealth is beyond our ken

On the stars in heaven he holds his court
And the moon comes down to kiss his fort

And because his support he does not withhold
I can write my verses so brash and bold

And caustic and bitter I can also sound
When, GHALIB, I feel this pain profound

98

Her aek baat pay kehtay ho tum keh too kya hay

Whenever I try to express my view
She promptly says, "But what're you?"

She becomes a lightening and a leaping fire
So you be careful, don't tell her your desire

She loves to listen and talk to my foe
And wherever she goes, she keeps him in tow

My clothes are sticking to my every sore
So about them bleeding I worry no more

She has burnt my heart as never before
Now what in the ashes is she looking for?

Your claim of love she won't recognize
Unless you bleed from your tearful eyes

O preacher, in the place you call paradise
Except for the wine there's nothing to entice

When I go to the bar, I do not chat
I simply sit and drink from the vat

But now I'm so weak I can hardly talk
And me, when I talk, people simply do mock

But since the king, GHALIB, is kind to me
To brag about it I always feel free

99

Ghair laen mehfil maen boasay jam kay

Oh, in her salon they all go and drink
But for me not a letter, my only link

I have my wounds; I have my pain
But this is my fate; I cannot complain

I've made her a name; I've given her fame
But they still say my love is only in name

My pleasure and business I try to combine
So even in Mecca I drink the wine

Oh, there's a trap not only in her hair
But her charming eye is also a snare

I've just now heard from the emperor's aide
That a complete recovery our ruler has made

And though I still can earn my livelihood
My love has made me, O GHALIB, no good

100
Phir is andaaz say bahaar aaie

O with great fanfare the spring is here
And the moon and the stars are coming to cheer

The bounty of God you cannot deny
Oh, what a beautiful way to beautify

With splendor the earth is flying high
It has become as dazzling as the glamorous sky

It's bright, and beautiful, and happy, and gay
And everything is green, and gone is the gray

In the springtime rain, having taken their showers
The flowers are admiring their fellow flowers

The breeze is bursting with fragrance divine
And the air is drunk with the smell of wine

And it's also great for the commonwealth
That the king has, GHALIB, regained his health

101
Kab wo sunta hay kahaani maeri

No wonder she would not hear my story
She knows it's sad, and gloomy, and gory

But with caution great she should proceed
She should be careful; I can bleed and bleed

To all my friends it appears like a breach
When they hear my muddled and frantic speech

My love has made me remote and numb
Oh, how forgetful have I now become

But I scare my foe; he lies very low
When like a torrent I flow and flow

But my callous gal I cannot reach
To her like a pebble I'm on the beach

My torrid wishes I cannot bear
Oh, I've no patience; I cannot forbear

Her mouth is like a red, red rose
Her pearl-like teeth it's made to enclose

But my love has made me so frail and weak
That my outlook , GHALIB, seems very, very bleak

102
Jis zakhm ki ho sakti ho tadbeer rafoo ki

My bleeding wounds O please don't sew
To my cowardly foe you ought to go

Oh, whenever I think of her rosy lip
The blood from my heart, it starts to drip

But my darling's nose is always in the air
For my moaning and groaning she does not care

She always keeps a dagger and a dart
And she keeps them ready for my breast and heart

And my gal, O GHALIB, is never contrite
All day, all night she's ready to fight

103
Chaahiay achhoun ko jitna chaahiay

If you only make friends with those who're nice
You'll surely be living in an earthly paradise

From the company of topers you should shrink
And too much liquor you should not drink

Your wayward heart you ought to control
Otherwise your flirting will take its toll

And don't go wild until it's spring
Let the flowers smile and the bluebirds sing

From your loving friend don't hide your face
And his tender affection please don't debase

And pay no attention to his terrible foe
For he likes to boast; he loves to crow

Wherever you go, you cause a riot
But your lover does like his peace and quiet

The woes of living he cannot bear
And since he can't die, you should see his despair

But he also loves the beautiful girls
And adores their eyes, their raven curls

But a beauty before he tries to hook
Says GHALIB, in the mirror he ought to look

104
Her qadam doori e manzil hay numaayaan mujh ko

My quest of attainment my goal exceeds
The further I go, it farther recedes

Her image from my eyes, it tries to flee
My sight gets dimmer, the harder I see

As the smoke from the fire tries to flee
My shadow wants to escape from me

Oh, no matter how much I try to explain
She cannot understand my grief or pain

When me into the desert my madness takes
From the fire of my heart the desert bakes

I'm like a shadow when I go in a trance
And all over my house I prance and dance

My trying to reach her is not a game
For I'm the moth, and she is the flame

This pain of parting I cannot fight
And when she's away, it's a total blight

But seeing my gal is such a delight
That I cannot believe my own eyesight

And in my heart there's so much fire
That, GHALIB, it can burn the world entire

105

Nuktacheen hay gham e dil is ko sunaa'ay na banay

Of sorrow my heart does always complain
But there's nothing I can do about this pain

Oh, how have I begged her to visit my slum
May be one day she'll relent and come

And though love for her is only a game
I wish at me she'll also take aim

In such a way carries her letters my foe
That if asked to show them, he cannot say no

And so delicate and dainty is my beautiful girl
That I'm afraid to touch even lightly her curl

To hide her face when she uses a veil
I cannot remove it; I always fail

I'd love her to come but dare not ask
Because I'm afraid she'll take me to task

This love for me is a crucifix
I don't know what to do, I'm in a fix

For love is a fire, O GHALIB, no doubt
You cannot start it; you can't put it out

106

Wo aa kay khaab maen taskeen e iztaraab toe day

She said in my dream one day she'll come
But what if insomnia I can't overcome

Once out of pity when she started to weep
With her wet eyelashes she stabbed me deep

Her beautiful smile I certainly miss
Though I know I do not deserve her kiss

O a fancy cup I do not demand
Just pour some wine in my empty hand

But, Ghalib, I'll have a heart attack
If once she said, "Come rub my back"

107
Feryaad ki koie lai naheen hay

I know, I know when I moan and groan
It has no pitch, it has no tone

They all say to me, "O what is up
And why is the tulip holding a cup?"

When God is present in everything
Then why there's a beggar; why there a king?

So let's not have any more confusion
This world is naught; it's just an illusion

In the end there's nothing there to explain
It's all subjective, this joy, this pain

And when our preacher rejects the wine
Little does he know that it's so divine

So, GHALIB, don't worry about anything
For nothing in the end is everything

108
Diya hay dil ager us ko, basher hay kya kahhiay

And though he's supposed to be my pal
It seems my courier loves also my gal

I've been asking and asking but he doesn't come
Of the Angel of Death oh, what has become?

And in her street he loves to roam
It seems my rival has made it his home

She is not only pretty but also smart
And knows exactly what's there in my heart

And when she sees me in her street
She opens the door and comes out to greet

But any good in love she fails to see
And value she does not my sincerity

When I raise the question of good and bad
She thinks I'm crazy; I'm totally mad

Of my wonderful verses she is not aware
And for poetic craft she does not care

But, GHALIB, you know I'm not so bad
Though I must confess I'm a little mad

109
Daekh ker der perda garm e daamanafshaani mujhay

In spite of all my efforts profound
To the flesh my soul is now tightly bound

Of her black enchanting eye, O Lord
She uses my heart to sharpen the sword

Though the tumult she causes does never cease
With herself my gal is always at peace

My pain and sorrow O how much I hate
But it is my destiny; it is my fate

And I feel like a lonely nightingale
Without his rose who can only wail

I thought it'd be peaceful after I die
But on Judgment Day I had to testify

She says she'll come and makes a date
But then she does not, and I wait and wait

But then one day when comes the spring
I forget my sorrow and start to sing

Then, GHALIB, I go to Yusuf, my brother
In handsomeness who's Joseph another

110
Huzoor e shah maen ahl e sukhan ki aazmaaish hay

The poets are there in the court of the king
To sing their songs like the birds in spring

And whether it's a Brahman or whether a Sheik
It is love and devotion that are at stake

While Joseph is honored and loved everywhere
What happens to Jacob people don't care

The girls do love to use their darts
They stab and jab their lovers' hearts

They show off their heights, and curves, and curls
To test their lovers, these beautiful girls

And in spite of his courage, his valor, his brawn
To a girl a lover is still a pawn

It's the job of a lover to always forbear
But whether it's fair, a girl doesn't care

And when a man is a captive of her curly hair
He has no choice but to grin and bear

And even if it's poison she wants him to swallow
His girl's instructions a lover must follow

And even if his beloved keeps the date
He still has to, GHALIB, contend with the fate

111

Kabhee naiki bhee us kay jee maen ger aa jay hay mujh say

Even when she's sorry about my plight
She wouldn't come to me; she's so contrite

And when I pull her, she pushes me away
Oh, this pulling and pushing are here to stay

When I tell her my tale, I come on strong
And I turn her off; it becomes too long

So she does not listen and I cannot talk
For I am a dove, and she is a hawk

When they come to see her from everywhere
Their looking at her I cannot bear

In the battle of love I feel dismay
I can neither leave nor can I stay

But I tell my despair when it becomes extreme
Don't let me lose O please my dream

And, GHALIB, this object of my love and lust
Even to God I cannot entrust

112
Baazeecha e atfaal hay dunya meray aagay

Everything in the world is in disarray
To me it looks like a child's play

The throne of Solomon isn't worth much
And the touch of Jesus is only a touch

The basis of being is greatly in doubt
And it's hard to guess what it's all about

And in the ocean I see nothing grand
And the desert to me is a handful of sand

And after drinking a little bit of wine
When I start to talk, I shine and shine

And I see in there the image divine
Whether it's a temple, a mosque, or a shrine

With my gal my life is full of bloom
And when she's away, there's nothing but gloom

Her cheek is shiny like a looking glass
Which gives my image a certain class

But I do feel a tinge of jealousy
When they rave about her in front of me

With the beautiful girls I like to be
And Juliets over Romeos do prefer me

With them my life is full of delight
And without them dark and bleak is my night

And in their absence I must concede
My poor heart breaks and I bleed and bleed

I know I'm weak, but as long as I can see
Please leave a little wine in front of me

And though I must say I sound rather mad
But, GHALIB, you know it's not that bad

113
Kahoun jo haal toe kehtay ho muddaa kahiay

When I go to her looking grim and gaunt
She promptly asks, "O what do you want?"

"You think I'm cruel" when she says to me
With her, I tell her, I can never disagree

Her proud glance is very like a dart
Oh, how I love it when it jabs my heart

And though my heart it's meant to destroy
To me her dart is a great source of joy

Be gentle to your gal even if a shrew
And don't be unkind if she's cruel to you

And seek some help to relieve your pain
But about your ailment do not complain

Do have some patience, and try to forbear
And live with your sorrow; do not despair

Be grateful to her if she takes your life
And when she stabs, do praise her knife

Be thankful to God that you have a gal
And what does it matter if she isn't your pal?

And go to the park and dance and sing
And enjoy the beautiful flowers of spring

And if in the end your goal you attain
"Thank God," says GHALIB, "and do not complain"

114
Ronay say aur ishq maen baibaak ho gaay

Instead of making my love obscene
My tears have washed it pure and clean

To buy some wine I've sold my gown
So now in the cup my pain I can drown

Oh, there was a time when I was a champ
But now I have become a beggar and a tramp

For it when moans the nightingale
The rose can't stay much hearty and hale

In the fire of love when a man does tread
He does not care if he's alive or dead

And when to his gal he goes to complain
She looks at him with great disdain

But one day, GHALIB, when he finally dies
Even his foes and rivals do mourn his demise

115
Jab tak dahaan e zakhm na paida keray koie

Before you tell her, "I love you so"
Your open wounds you'll have to show

And Romeo has his great despair
Because of the curls of Juliet's hair

You can't have love without the ache
Your heart must yearn; it also must break

The laws of love you cannot defy
You sit all night and cry and cry

And if your sorrow you cannot bear
The clothes on your body you then have to tear

If you can't get your rose and feel lovelorn
With your tears of blood you nourish the thorn

And if one day with her you can be
You'll be dazzled, and her you won't see

And if your madness you cannot subdue
Everyone will throw stones at you

If you invite her, and she doesn't come
You just accept it, and do not be glum

But if your sorrow gets harder to bear
Don't get depressed, and do not despair

And if it doesn't turn out the way you planned
Don't bang your head against your hand

And GHALIB says if it gets much worse
Your shattered heart you put in your verse

116
Ibn e Meryam hua keray koie

She has breath of Jesus and a divine touch
So my asking for cure is not that much

With a simple touch she can cure your ill
But with a single look she can also kill

Her brow is a bow; her glance a dart
She can jab, and stab, and wound your heart

O you should see her, whenever she talks
No one can speak, and everyone gawks

In a fit of madness but when I talk
I know it is nothing but poppycock

So if it is some evil, do not hear
And say good things, and do not fear

If someone is lost, do show him the way
And pardon those who have gone astray

And try to help people who are in need
And be their friend and a friend indeed

And those who waver, help them decide
And show them the way, and be their guide

And GHALIB tells us don't ever complain
And try to smile whenever you've pain

117
Hazaaroun khaahishaen aisi keh her khaahish pay dam niklay

O wishes in my heart I've an awful lot
And for each fulfilled, there're ten that are not

But the people who offer me their sympathy
In love they've suffered far more than me

From drinking a lot I do not shrink
And it was I who taught Jum how to drink

If you cannot write, I'll not misquote
And write with care to your love your note

Yes, Adam was expelled from Eden I know
But how from her house oh, she asked me to go

Why should she worry about blood in my tears?
It's not her fault; I've had it for years

The twists and turns of her golden hair
If ever she lost them, her lovers will despair

To kill her lover she uses her knife
But also with a touch she restores his life

And, GHALIB, our preacher I've begun to doubt
For often from the bar I see him coming out

118
Jis ja naseem shaanakash e zulf e yaar hay

When flies in the breeze her curly hair
The musk of Tatar you smell everywhere

And when from her face she lifts the veil
The hearts go crazy in every dale

The flowers do blossom in mead and vale
And sings his song the nightingale

The birds and the flowers look woebegone
They think, when she leaves, that the summer is gone

Every grain of dirt is under her command
So at her call lose deserts their sand

Oh, she is so lovely, so charming, so fair
That they come to see her from everywhere

Her beautiful face they greatly admire
And their hearts and eyes are full of desire

If she says she'll come when they invite
They wait for her all day, all night

But with her absence they cannot cope
Their hearts all break; they lose their hope

And, GHALIB, they then cry and cry
And become so dejected they all want to die

119
Aaiena kuin na doom keh tamaasha kahaen jisay

If believe me you don't, look in the glass
Like you in this world there isn't a lass

When I think of you, I think of a rose
My heart does crave, and wild it goes

This love and yearning for me are the same
And the endless waiting is their other name

Oh, I'm a lonely stranger in your city
Look at my plight, and please take pity

It's dying to see you, my tearful eye
How long, how long will you make it cry?

It needs to be happy, this heart of mine
The spring is here, so give it some wine

And you know our GHALIB, he's a wonderful teacher
He tells us we should not worry about the preacher

120
Shabnam ba gul e laala na khaali zay ada hay

On the face of tulip the drops of dew
Oh, what a lovely sight; what a wonderful view

Her beautiful face when it does not see
You should see my heart and its agony

I tell my heart that it is not a game
For it's the moth, and she is the flame

And when the mirror sees her gorgeous face
It falls in love with her beauty and grace

And in her garden the nightingale
To mourn her absence it only can wail

But when she's caustic, and bitter, and tart
It's in a quandary, my poor little heart

The bondage of love is all too strong
And it becomes more binding as you go along

The victims of love can never complain
They learn to live with the dagger and chain

But she's more precious than the sun and the moon
And we lovers enjoy her benevolent boon

Oh, if for our sins we're going to be hit
Laud us also for those we could not commit

So our cruel world we should not mind
For, GHALIB, our Lord is generous and kind

121
Manzoor thi yeh shakl tajalli ko noor ki

O the Burning Bush you will not chase
If you only could see my darling's face

When my bleeding heart they saw in my grave
For it the houris started to crave

O preacher, my wine is also divine
And nobody can drink your heavenly wine

On the Judgment Day when I left my grave
She told me I was dead, and I should behave

The spring has come, and the flowers are there
And the birds are singing and flying everywhere

Oh, these beautiful idols, please don't smash
They were once in Mecca, they are not trash

The ways of God you should not discount
And like Moses you ought to go to the mount

And whenever you talk, you should be kind
For if you are rude, people do mind

And believe me, GHALIB, I'll give anything
If takes me with him on his journey the king

122
Gham khhaanay maen boda dil e naakaam bohat hay

My heart can't bear this sorrow and pain
No more from drinking can I afford to abstain

O maid of the bar, if you can't spare wine
Give me some dregs; for me they are fine

It's so nice in here; I like my prison
For there are no predators where I am in

O preacher, your piety I cannot afford
I don't like punishment; I don't want reward

The people who think that they're so wise
To follow convention they always advise

Oh, business and pleasure I'd like to combine
When I go to Mecca, I'll carry some wine

And though I'm certain she will resist
She'll have to be nice, I'm going to insist

If the Angel of Death does come to me
I can't go, I'll tell him, I'm just too busy

And though as a poet I don't have fame
To be notorious, GHALIB, I can certainly claim

123
Muddat hoie hay yaar ko mehmaan kiay huay

Oh, it has been long since she was here
And we sat and drank our bubbly beer

Part by part I'm assembling my heart
To make it ready for her deadly dart

It has been a while since I felt despair
And ripped my clothes and tore my hair

But somehow now I've a burning desire
And all of a sudden I'm breathing fire

My heart again has an open sore
And it's scared of salt as never before

My eyes are shedding the tears of blood
And are afraid of causing a veritable flood

My eyes do want to see her face
And my heart is yearning for her beauty and grace

To look for her it will go anywhere
And what happens to it my heart doesn't care

Its yearning and craving it cannot control
For it belongs to her with all its soul

And tulips and roses it wants to see
And with the nightingale it'd like to be

That she really cares it wants to believe
So a letter from her it'd like to receive

And on her terrace when she is there
Its love for her it'd like to declare

And with mascara, from her long eyelashes
It wants to get some jabs and slashes

And after she has taken a cup of wine
It wants to see on her face the shine

Its reach to her house it wants to extend
Of her terrible doorman by becoming a friend

And nothing would give it more delight
Than to think of her all day, all night

So, GHALIB, be careful with my woeful heart
And touch it not, for it'll fall apart

124
Naveed e amn hay baidaad e dost jaan kay liay

Oh, cruelty and malice, she has them all
But then she is also a beautiful doll

I can't lose it all when my heart does bleed
For blood for my tears I also do need

From the woes of life I want to be free
So this eternal life is not for me

My peace of mind she does subvert
She's so very coy; she's such a flirt

Me, like all lovers, she likes to test
But I don't succeed though I try my best

Oh, I'm her captive; I like my prison
But I also miss home, when there I'm in

And though for him I've great regard
He thinks I'm a tramp, my prison guard

And though there're millions and millions of ways
My verses lack power to fittingly praise

Our T. H. Khan is a chosen man
And God is also his ardent fan

And when I try to pronounce his name
My tongue does say it with great acclaim

His grasp on thing is so complete
That the sky comes down to kiss his feet

And when they see him holding the helm
People feel happy throughout his realm

To do him justice is very, very tough
For in his praise you can't say enough

So, GHALIB, to everyone I issue a call
O come and admire him; come one, come all

Read Free

English and Urdu translation in VERSE of the Persian odes of KHUSRO and HAFIZ
and
English translation in VERSE of the Urdu odes of GHALIB
by
Logging on to URL: www.writing.com/authors/khalmeed
Searching through Google under: Khalid Hameed Shaida

Buy Books
amazon. com and other etailers

1. Khusro, the Indian Orpheus, a hundred odes
2. Hafiz, the Voice of God, a hundred odes
3. Hafiz, Drunk with God, selected odes
4. Ghalib, the Indian Beloved, Urdu odes

Suraj, 6/A Naseeruddin Road, Islampura, Lahore, Pakistan.
Email: <u>surajquarterly@yahoo.com</u>

1. Dr. Khalid Hameed Shaida Number I with English and Urdu Translation of Ghalib
2. Dr. Khalid Hameed Shaida Number II with English and Urdu Translation of Hafiz
3. Khusro aur Iqbal with English and Urdu Translation of Khusro and Iqbal

Write to the translator: Khalid Hameed Shaida, MD
2208 Lakeway Drive, Friendswood, TX 77546, USA
Email: khalmeed@aol.com